# *Contents*



Nos. 1 and 5 are taken from Anna Magdalena Bach's manuscript book of 1725.

Nos. 2, 3 and 4 appeared in the *Gesangbuch* published in Leipzig in 1736 by Georg Christian Schemelli; this was a collection of 'Spiritual Songs, Old and New' of which the musical editor was Johann Sebastian Bach.

# FIVE SPIRITUAL SONGS
## (Geistliche Lieder)

English translations
by PETER PEARS

J. S. BACH
Realized by BENJAMIN BRITTEN

## 1. Gedenke doch, mein Geist, zurücke
Consider then, my soul unwary

man mich wird zur Ruh' be - glei - ten, auf dass ich klüg - lich
soon e - ter - nal rest a - waits thee, pre - pare thy - self for
ster - ben mag.
death as well.
Schreib'
In -
p
die - ses Wort in Herz und Brust: 'Ge - den - ke, dass du
- scribe these words with - in thy heart: 'Re - call how near to
ster - ben musst'.
death thou art'.
dim.
pp

# 2. Kommt, Seelen, dieser Tag

Come, celebrate this morn

cresc.
Heut' hat der heil' - ge Geist viel
Up - on this ve - ry day the
der stim - me mit uns ein und
Let him u - nite with us in
cresc.
Hel - den aus - ge - rüst't, so be - tet, dass er
saints were arm'd with love, So pray the Ho - ly
prei - se Got - tes Treu', sie ist an die - sem
prai - ses strong and true To God, the glo - rious
f
f
auch die Her - zen hier be - grüsst.
Ghost may bless us from a - bove.
Fest und al - le Mor - gen neu!
King, e - ter - nal, e - ver new.

# 3. Liebster Herr Jesu

Dearest Lord Jesus

von der be - schwer - li - chen, angst - vol - len Welt!
far from this world with its bur - dens of ill.
und mei - ner bit - - te - ren Trä - nen so satt!
bit - ter - ly weep - ing, I long to de - part.
mf
dim.
Komm doch, Herr Je - su, wo bleibst du so lan - ge? wo
Come then, Lord Je - sus; ah why dost thou tar - ry? ah
dim.
pp
bleibst du so lan - ge? Komm doch, mir wird hier auf
why dost thou tar - ry? Come and re - lease me from
Er - den so ban - ge, so ban - ge! ban - - - ge!
bond - age so wea - ry, so wea - ry. wea - - - ry.
pp
1
2
rall.

# 4. Komm, süsser Tod

Come, soothing death

The original is in C minor

cresc.
mü - de. Ach, komm, ich wart' auf dich,
shri - ven. Ah come, I wait for thee,
ste - hen. Es ist ja nun voll - bracht,
greet thee. Now fades the day's pale light;
cresc.
dim.
komm bald und füh - re mich, drück' mir die
Come to de - li - ver me, Ah let my
Welt, da - rum gu - te Nacht, mein' Au - gen
World, take my last 'good - night'. My wea - ry
dim.
p (pp)
Au - gen zu. Komm, sel' - ge Ruh'!
eye - lids close, Come, sweet re - pose!
schliess' ich zu. Komm, sel' - ge Ruh'!
eye - lids close, Come, sweet re - pose!
2nd time
p (pp)
5
Ped.

# 5. Bist du bei mir

If thou art near

Attributed to G. H. Stölzel

zum Ster - ben und zu mei - ner Ruh', zum Ster-ben und zu mei-ner
to death and my e - ter - nal rest, to death and my e-ter-nal
pp
Ped. Ped. Ped. Ped. etc.
Ruh'. Ach, wie ver - gnügt wär' so mein
rest. Ah, what de - light were such a
p
En - de, es drück-ten dei-ne schö - nen Hän - de mir
dy - ing! I feel up - on my eye - lids ly - ing thy
pp
Ped. Ped. Ped. Ped.
die ge-treu - en Au - gen zu. Ach, wie ver - gnügt
ten - der hands, with com - fort blest. Ah, what de - light
p
Ped. etc.

(Aldeburgh
June 1969)